OCEANS AND SEAS!

Anita Yasuda

Illustrated by Tom Casteel

Titles in the **Explore Waterways** Set

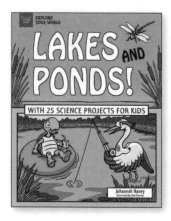

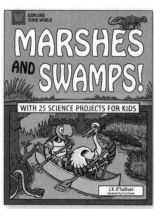

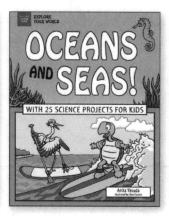

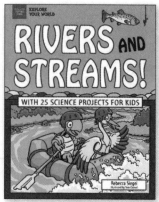

Check out more titles at www.nomadpress.net

Nomad Press
A division of Nomad Communications
10 9 8 7 6 5 4 3 2 1

This book was manufactured by Versa Press,
East Peoria, Illinois
November 2018, Job #J18-09202

ISBN Softcover: 978-1-61930-698-1
ISBN Hardcover: 978-1-61930-696-7

Educational Consultant, Marla Conn

Questions regarding the ordering of this book should be addressed to
Nomad Press
2456 Christian St.
White River Junction, VT 05001
www.nomadpress.net

CONTENTS

Interested in primary sources? Look for this icon. Use a smartphone or tablet app to scan the QR code and explore more! Photos are also primary sources because a photograph takes a picture at the moment something happens.

You can find a list of URLs on the Resources page. Try searching the internet with the Keyword Prompts to find other helpful sources.

KEYWORD PROMPTS

oceans and seas

WHAT LIVES IN OCEANS AND SEAS?

Many plants and animals make their homes in oceans and seas. Here is a glimpse of just a few—you'll meet many more in the pages of this book!

BLUE WHALES are the largest animals known to have ever lived on Earth.

SEA OTTERS have two layers of fur to keep them warm.

PHYTOPLANKTON absorb carbon dioxide and release oxygen.

SEAGRASS isn't actually grass. It's more closely related to lilies that grow on land.

INTRODUCTION

WHAT ARE OCEANS AND SEAS?

Imagine piloting your own submarine. You're eager to grab the control stick. You push it forward, and the bright yellow sub picks up speed. Your heart races as you plunge into the largest ecosystem on Earth—the ocean! There is no turning back now!

Outside the large glass window, a school of blue striped fish swirls past. Leaf-like creatures are beating their fins like birds. And are those balls of dancing jelly? You steer the sub past towering rocks covered with blankets of orange sponges.

WORDS ⊚ KNOW

ecosystem: a community of living and nonliving things and their environment. Living things are plants, animals, and insects. Nonliving things are soil, rocks, and water.

ocean: a large body of salt water that surrounds the earth's continents.

1

OCEANS AND SEAS!

Down, down you go, until you're nearly at the bottom of the ocean. What could that noise be? You peer into the inky blackness. Is that an eye the size of a dinner plate looking back at you? Your adventure in the ocean has begun!

WHAT IS THE OCEAN?

Salt water covers 75 percent of the earth's surface. This water is contained in the earth's huge global ocean. The ocean is so big that it wraps all the way around our planet! Whether you splash in the waves off Maine, surf in Australia, or hike along a coastline in the Arctic, you're in the same world ocean. That's how large the ocean is! It's easy to see why the earth's nickname is the "Blue Planet."

A PICTURE OF EARTH FROM SPACE IN 1972
CREDIT: NASA/APOLLO 17 CREW

When you look at a world map, you see seven large continents. The continents divide the ocean into five main areas of salt water. These are the Atlantic, Pacific, Indian, Arctic, and Southern Oceans.

WHAT DOES THE OCEAN DO WHEN IT PASSES THE SHORE?

It waves!

The largest of the five oceans is the Pacific Ocean. It covers more than 60 million square miles. That's enormous! If the continents were puzzle pieces, they could all fit in the Pacific Ocean.

An area around the Pacific Ocean is famous for volcanoes and earthquakes. It's called the Ring of Fire. There are more than 450 active volcanoes here. The Pacific Ocean has more volcanoes than anywhere else.

The second-largest ocean is the Atlantic Ocean. It flows between the icy North and South Poles and covers 31 million square miles. The Atlantic Ocean coastline zigs and zags, forming many natural harbors and ports. The Atlantic is the busiest ocean.

DID YOU KNOW?

The Pacific, Atlantic, and Indian Oceans are home to the biggest fish in the world—the whale shark. It can weigh up to 75,000 pounds and is covered with tooth-like scales.

The warm waters of the Indian Ocean flow past more than 37 countries. This ocean takes its name from one of these countries—India. The Indian Ocean covers slightly more than 28 million square miles. In the winter, monsoon winds bring warm, dry weather across the Indian Ocean. If you sail these waters in the summer, you will find wet and stormy weather.

OCEANS AND SEAS!

The icy-cold Arctic Ocean is at the northernmost tip of the world. It's named after the great bear constellation, Ursa Major, in the Northern Hemisphere. The word *arktos* means "bear" in Greek. The Arctic Ocean covers 5 million square miles. If you ever visit, you'll see ice floating on the ocean for most of the year.

The Southern Ocean surrounds the continent of Antarctica like a giant donut. Its waters flow across 7 million square miles. This ocean is freezing. With temperatures between 28 and 50 degrees Fahrenheit (–2 to 10 degrees Celsius), the Southern Ocean is the coldest ocean in the world. It is known for furious winds that can blow more than 100 miles per hour.

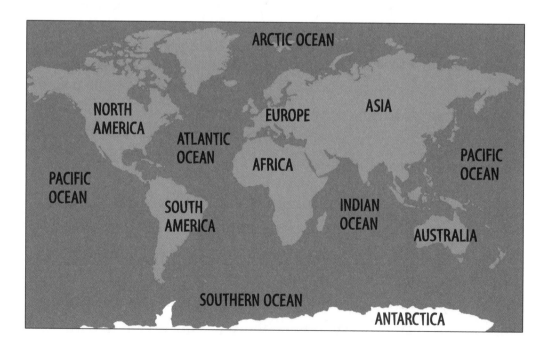

4

OCEAN STORIES

Have you heard the story about the sea monster? It reared its terrible head above the waves and then . . . *snap*! The sailor was gone, disappeared without a trace.

People have been telling tall tales about the ocean for hundreds of years. These stories were exciting to hear, but they weren't true. People could only guess what was in the ocean because they did not have the technology to explore it. To explain what they couldn't see or understand, people told stories. Can you think of other stories that were created to explain strange things?

These stories described sunken cities and sea gods. Some storytellers frightened audiences with tales of wicked mermaids and sailor-eating serpents.

One example of an ocean tale comes from Japan. This folk story tells of a fisherman named Urashima Taro. After the fisherman does a good deed, he rides on the back of a turtle to a magnificent underwater palace. He lives here happily with a beautiful princess for hundreds of years.

Other stories aren't so peaceful. For example, in Norse mythology, there is a giant serpent called Jormungand.

WORDS TO KNOW

technology: the tools, methods, and systems used to solve a problem or do work.

Norse: people from Denmark, Norway, and Sweden.

mythology: a collection of traditional stories, either truthful or exaggerated, that are often focused on historical events.

DID YOU KNOW?

The word *ocean* comes from the Greek word *keanos*, meaning "great stream around the earth."

5

geography: the features of a place, such as mountains and rivers.

marine: having to do with the ocean.

BCE: put after a date, BCE stands for Before Common Era and counts down to zero. CE stands for Common Era and counts up from zero. These non-religious terms correspond to BC and AD. This book was printed in 2018 CE.

WORDS TO KNOW

The gods throw the serpent into the ocean to get rid of it. But the serpent is not destroyed. Instead, it feasts on whales until it grows so big it circles the world. Jormungand becomes so hungry that it bites its tail!

These ancient stories show us that the ocean was once considered a strange and mysterious place. While there is still much to learn about the ocean, we have discovered a lot about its geography, plants, and animals by experimenting and observing.

STUDYING THE OCEAN

One of the first people to write about marine life was a man named Aristotle. He was a Greek scientist and thinker who lived from 384 to 322 BCE.

Aristotle studied the world around him at a time when many ancient Greeks looked to the gods to explain the world. They worshipped the god Poseidon, who was the ruler of the sea. The Greeks thought Poseidon was moody. They said that when Poseidon was angered, he whisked the sea into a powerful storm.

Aristotle knew these stories, but he wanted to use science to study the ocean and its plants and animals. He spent many hours exploring tidepools. He studied what tidepool animals ate and drew pictures of how they moved.

Aristotle created a classification system for the animals he observed. Movement was one method Aristotle used to classify animals. His system placed animals into swimming, walking, and flying groups. He wrote down the names of more than 1,400 marine animals. Many of these names are ones that we still use today.

tidepool: a pool of ocean water that remains after the tide goes out.

classification system: a way of organizing things in groups.

sea: a large body of salt water that is mostly surrounded by land.

WORDS to KNOW

WHAT IS A SEA?

A sea is a body of salty water. It's mostly surrounded by land. The largest inland sea in the world is the Mediterranean Sea.

MEET EUGENIE!

Eugenie Clark (1922–2015) was nicknamed "Shark Lady." Can you imagine why? She loved sharks! When she was a kid, her favorite place to go was the New York Aquarium. She used to wonder what it would be like to swim with the creatures she saw there. As a grownup, Clark became a scientist who studied fish. She took more than 70 dives in the ocean. She died eight months after her last scuba dive at the age of 92!

7

The Mediterranean Sea separates Europe from Africa. Deep beneath its waves is the biggest underwater volcano in Europe—the Marsili Seamount. The Marsili rises 9,800 feet from the seafloor.

The Mediterranean Sea flows into the Atlantic Ocean. Some seas do not flow directly into the ocean. For example, the Black Sea flows into the Aegean Sea, which flows into the Mediterranean Sea before reaching the Atlantic Ocean.

You can see the Mediterranean Sea, Aegean Sea, and Black Sea in this photograph.

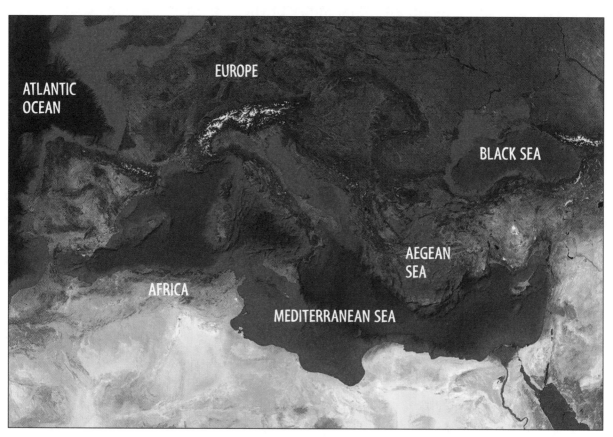

CREDIT: NASA

8

One sea off the coast of Florida is different from all other seas in the world. The Sargasso Sea is part of the Atlantic Ocean. It doesn't have any land boundaries. Instead, it is a large area of floating seaweed created by the ocean currents around it.

Have you ever licked the water off your face at the ocean? It must have tasted salty. The Dead Sea has almost 10 times as much salt as the ocean. It's so salty, that you can easily float on it.

This book will take you through colorful coral reefs and underwater forests. You'll learn how the ocean keeps us alive and you'll discover the ocean's influence on weather and climate. You'll also meet strange sea creatures covered in tooth-like scales and others that can change color. Plus, there will be water experiments to do, volcanoes to make, secret messages to send, and currents to study.

Would you like to climb the tallest mountain or journey through the deepest canyon on Earth? How about taking a selfie with the largest mammal in the world? On this journey, it's all possible. Let's explore oceans and seas!

current: the steady flow of water or air in one direction.

coral reef: an underwater ecosystem that grows in warm ocean waters and is home to millions of creatures. Corals are tiny animals that build shells around themselves.

climate: weather patterns over a long period of time.

mammal: an animal such as a human, dog, or cat. Mammals are born live, feed milk to their young, and usually have hair or fur.

WORDS TO KNOW

DID YOU KNOW?

Some bodies of water called seas are not part of an ocean. They are surrounded by land. The Dead Sea is a body of salty water between Israel and Jordan. It doesn't connect to any ocean.

GOOD SCIENCE PRACTICES

Every good scientist keeps a science journal. On page 12, you'll find instructions to make a notebook to use as your science journal. Write down your ideas, observations, and comparisons as you read this book.

For each project in this book, make and use a scientific method worksheet, like the one shown here. Scientists use the scientific method to keep their experiments organized. A scientific method worksheet will help you keep track of your observations and results.

Each chapter of this book begins with a question to help guide your exploration of oceans and seas.

Scientific Method Worksheet
Question: What problem are we trying to solve?
Research: What information is already known?
Hypothesis/Prediction: What do I think the answer will be?
Equipment: What supplies do I need?
Method: What steps will I follow?
Results: What happened and why?

? **INVESTIGATE!**

Why do you think Earth is nicknamed the Blue Planet?

Keep the question in your mind as you read the chapter. Record your thoughts, questions, and observations in your science journal. At the end of each chapter, use your science journal to think of answers to the question. Does your answer change as you read the chapter?

INVESTIGATE THE WORLD

The world map can look like puzzle pieces. You can decide which shapes best represent each continent and put together your own map. How are all the oceans connected?

1 Cut the blue paper in half lengthwise and attach the sheets end to end with clear tape. Use the ruler to draw a dotted horizontal line across the middle to represent the equator.

2 Cut out geometric shapes, including triangles, rectangles, and diamonds. Use the shapes to create the continents. Look at the picture on page 4 to see the shape of the continents.

3 Glue the shapes to the blue paper and label them: North America, South America, Asia, Africa, Antarctica, Europe, and Australia.

TRY THIS! With permission from an adult, do some online research on two seas. Label their locations on the map.

4 Label the oceans: Pacific, Atlantic, Indian, Southern, and Arctic.

THINK ABOUT IT! What is the closest ocean to you? What is the farthest ocean away from you? Have you seen any of the oceans in real life? What are they like?

OCEAN JOURNAL

Captain James Cook (1728–1779) was a famous British explorer. On his journey to the Arctic Ocean, he kept a journal and recorded his observations about Arctic ice. Today, scientists use Captain Cook's notes to understand how sea ice in the Arctic is changing. You, too, can record your observations in a science journal. Who will read about your discoveries in the future?

SUPPLIES

* ✳ 3 pieces yellow paper, 9 by 12 inches
* ✳ 3-hole puncher
* ✳ brad
* ✳ 21 pieces of paper, 9 by 12 inches, including some black paper
* ✳ pencil
* ✳ pencil compass
* ✳ scissors
* ✳ glue stick
* ✳ chalk or your school photo
* ✳ crayons
* ✳ black yarn

1 For the journal covers, place two yellow sheets of paper together and make three holes along one edge. Set to one side.

2 From the third piece of yellow paper, cut out the top of the submarine and glue in place as shown in the illustration. Attach the periscope with a brad so that you can raise it up or lower it down.

3 Use your pencil compass to draw a circle on one sheet of black paper for the submarine window. Glue it near the top of the front cover. Use chalk to add details to the window or glue your school photo to the window. At the bottom of the cover, add an ocean scene with your crayons.

WORDS ⛭ KNOW

periscope: a long tube with two mirrors used in submarines to see above the surface of the ocean.

GPS: stands for Global Positioning System, a network of satellites that can be used to find your location on Earth.

PROJECT!

4 Take the rest of the black paper for the inside of your journal. Punch three holes along one side of the papers. Center the pages between the covers.

5 Finish your journal with the yarn by threading it through the holes to sew the covers and inside papers together. Go back and forth two or three times so your binding is strong. Tie the yarn off when you're done. Your journal is ready to use!

THINK ABOUT IT!

Captain Cook had to keep his journal safe even as he sailed through terrible weather! How can you keep your journal safe when you are investigating oceans?

AHOY!

Captain Cook sailed thousands of miles across oceans that no one had ever explored before. And he did this in the days before GPS! He made many observations of the people he met, the plants he found, and the animals he encountered.

   You can see and read his journals at these websites.

KEYWORD PROMPTS
NLA Cook journal 🔍

KEYWORD PROMPTS
Captain Cook journals 🔍

CHAPTER 1

OCEAN CONNECTIONS

Beaches are a great place to be in the summer. You can float and splash in waves. You can ride a surfboard and buzz around in a boat on the ocean surface. A mask and snorkel let you explore underwater.

Have you ever wanted to find pirate treasure? Maybe you imagined a chest bursting with gold coins! It turns out, the ocean has many kinds of other treasures. The ocean is an amazing source of energy, natural resources, and food.

 INVESTIGATE!

What three objects in your home came from an ocean resource?

RENEWABLE ENERGY

You use energy every day. It powers your computer and the lights in your room. Have you ever wondered where this energy comes from?

Energy comes from both renewable and nonrenewable sources. Renewable resources are ones that don't get used up or pollute the environment. The sun, the wind, and the ocean are all renewable energy sources.

Energy can be harvested by the movement of the ocean's tides. Have you ever noticed the tide going in or out at the beach? Tides are caused by the pull of the moon and sun on the earth.

Some countries, including the United States and Canada, harness tidal energy to produce electricity. The largest tidal energy project in the world is in eastern Canada, in the Bay of Fundy. This special place has the highest tides in the world. The water level here can change more than four stories, or 53 feet!

natural resource: something found in nature that is useful to humans, such as water to drink, trees to burn and build with, and fish to eat.

renewable: a resource such as wind that people can never run out of.

nonrenewable: a resource such as coal that, once used, is gone forever.

tidal: having to do with the daily rise and fall of ocean water.

WORDS TO KNOW

LOW TIDE

HIGH TIDE

MOON'S GRAVITATIONAL PULL

Turbines in the Bay of Fundy act like giant underwater windmills. The blades within the turbines rotate as the tides roll in and out. Power cables connect the turbines to the power grid. The energy produced powers 500 homes. In the future, it might power 100,000 homes.

YOU CAN WALK AROUND ON THE BOTTOM OF THE BAY OF FUNDY AT LOW TIDE!
CREDIT: PETER C (CC BY 2.0)

NONRENEWABLE ENERGY

While renewable energy sources don't get used up, nonrenewable energy sources, such as fossil fuels, will someday run out. Oil and gas are examples of fossil fuels. They formed from dead plants and animals that settled at the bottom of the ocean millions of years ago. These dead creatures eventually turned into an oil that can be burned for energy. When people burn fossil fuels, they release gases into the atmosphere that cause pollution.

16

AN OIL RIG OFF THE COAST OF BRAZIL
CREDIT: AGÊNCIA BRASIL (CC BY 3.0B)

WHERE DO GHOSTS LIKE TO SWIM?

The Dead Sea.

More than one-third of the oil and gas in the world comes from the ocean. People dig deep into the ocean floor to get at this trapped oil. Oil companies build platforms in the ocean called oil rigs.

The Thunder Horse rig in the Gulf of Mexico is the world's largest oil platform—it's the size of three football fields! A massive drill on the platform crunches through 3 miles of mud and rock to reach the oil. Thunder Horse produces up to 250,000 barrels of oil a day. This amount of oil could power a city the size of Miami, Florida, for one month!

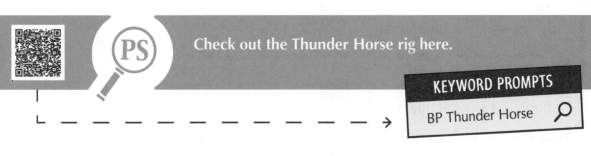

PS

Check out the Thunder Horse rig here.

KEYWORD PROMPTS

BP Thunder Horse 🔍

MIGHTY MINERALS

People use minerals to make jewelry and build homes. They also eat minerals—salt! Salt is one of the most important minerals in the ocean.

About 5,000 years ago, people along the coast of China began taking salt out of the ocean. They boiled ocean water until nothing remained but salt. They used the salt to preserve food, such as eggs, and to add flavor to food.

In other areas of the world, people used evaporation in a different way. They left ocean water to evaporate in shallow pools. The result was the same. The sun shone down on the pool and the liquid turned to a gas until just salt remained.

THEN & NOW

THEN: Nearly 2,000 years ago, the ancient Romans built a ship large enough to carry up to 600 tons. That is four times the weight of a blue whale.

NOW: The world's largest container ship can carry more than 21,000 containers, or 210 thousand tons.

VACUUMING THE OCEAN FLOOR

The ocean floor is rich in other types of minerals. Companies mine the ocean's muddy floor for precious minerals such as gold and diamonds. One company in Africa has a floating diamond mine off the coast of Namibia. The company uses 300-foot-long ships with vacuum-cleaner-like suction pipes to take samples of sediment from the seafloor. Back on the ship, workers sift the sediment and remove the diamonds. The sediment is then put back in the ocean.

sediment: bits of rock, sand, or dirt.

seaweed: a type of plant that grows in the ocean.

nori: dried seaweed often used to wrap sushi.

organism: a living thing, such as an animal or a plant.

WORDS TO KNOW

HAVE SOME SEAWEED!

Have you ever eaten seaweed? Cooks use seaweed in noodles, cookies, and bread. One shop in China uses seaweed in donuts!

Sushi chefs wrap sheets of nori around raw fish. Nori is a seaweed that's grown on large ocean farms. Seaweed farms are common in some countries, including China, Japan, and South Korea.

DID YOU KNOW?

Coral reefs are like medicine cabinets. Many organisms that live on the reefs are being used in medicines.

(PS) Watch a film about people who harvest seaweed in Maine. Would you like this kind of job?

KEYWORD PROMPTS

PBS seaweed harvesting

19

WORDS TO KNOW

alginate: a seaweed extract that makes foods thicker.

algae: a simple organism found in water that is like a plant but without roots, stems, or leaves.

Seaweed has many uses in food because it contains alginates. Alginates make foods thicker. Companies use alginates in many different foods, such as jelly, milkshakes, and ice cream. Your shampoo, body lotion, and toothpaste may also contain seaweed!

People have had a long and useful relationship with the ocean! In the next chapter, we'll look at some of the history of ocean exploration.

? CONSIDER AND DISCUSS

It's time to consider and discuss: What three objects in your home came from an ocean resource?

MARVELOUS MEDICINES

In the last 40 years, scientists have discovered more than 30,000 new chemicals from ingredients beneath the waves. Algae, for example, is used in medicines that fight serious diseases, including some types of cancer. Scientists also use chemicals found in spiny starfish, corals, and sponges in medicines. For almost 20 years, Dr. Shirley Pomponi has been working as a scientific diver and collecting sea sponges. Scientists are studying how chemicals in sea sponges can help people. So far, scientists have discovered 8,000 new chemicals from sponges!

Maybe one day the chemicals found in sea sponges will help cure cancer! **Find out about Dr. Shirley Pomponi's work collecting sponges at this website.**

KEYWORD PROMPTS

Smithsonian Pomponi 🔍

SUPPLIES

* science journal and pencil
* timer

SEAWEED SCAVENGER HUNT

How many seaweed products are there in your house? It's time to become a seaweed sleuth!

1 Start a scientific method worksheet and write down a prediction. Which room will have the most products containing seaweed?

2 This is a 10-minute challenge, so set the timer to 10 minutes. Begin with the refrigerator. Take out an item and look at the ingredient label. If you see alginate, carrageenan, or beta-carotene, that's seaweed.

DID YOU KNOW?

Ancestors of the horseshoe crab lived 450 million years ago! This crab spends most of the year in the deep sea. It only comes ashore in the spring to mate. This is when the female horseshoe crab lays about 90,000 eggs! But only a few of these eggs live to adulthood. Scientists use chemicals from the horseshoe crab to make medicines such as the flu shot.

3 When you find a seaweed extract, write the name of the product in your science journal. Continue until you hear the buzzer. Repeat steps two and three for your food cabinets and the bathroom.

4 Compare your results with your prediction. What item was the most surprising?

TRY THIS! Select four products. Read the ingredients list again. Do some products contain more than one seaweed extract? Write your results in your science journal.

PROJECT!

CARGO SHIPS

Empty cargo ships carry water called ballast **to make them stable. The ships release the water when they arrive at their destinations. Sometimes, the ballast contains organisms hitching a ride to a new place. See how ballast works in this activity.**

1 Start a scientific method worksheet in your science journal and write down a prediction. What do you think will happen when you place coins in the water?

2 Place the clear bowl on the baking sheet. Using the measuring jug, fill the bowl to the rim with water.

3 Place one coin into the bowl. Add more coins one at a time. As you add each coin, write down your observations in your science journal.

4 Empty out the water and coins. Fill the bowl with water again and sprinkle with grated orange peel. The grated orange peel represents plants and animals not native to an area.

5 Rest the sieve over the mixing bowl. Pour the water through the sieve. What do you see in the sieve and in the water? Write down your observations.

WORDS TO KNOW

ballast: something used to make a ship more stable, such as water or sand.

trade: the buying, selling, or exchange of goods and services between countries.

goods: things to use or sell.

cargo ship: a ship used to carry goods and materials from one port to another.

species: a group of living things that are closely related and can produce young.

22

SUPER SHIPPING

When you start eating your school lunch, do you think about how fruits, vegetables, and bread arrived at your school? Most food spends some time traveling by ship. Nearly 90 percent of everything we buy, from food to sneakers, arrives in the United States on a ship. The ocean is incredibly important in international trade. Goods are shipped in large metal boxes called containers. The containers are carried by cargo ships. At any time, as many as 50,000 cargo ships could be on the oceans.

THINK ABOUT IT! Ballast contains tiny hitchhikers—plants and animals from other countries. They often compete for resources with local organisms. How effective was straining the water in removing these hitchhikers? Can you think of a more effective way?

TRY THIS! With help from an adult, research a marine plant or animal that is not originally from your country. These are invasive **species** if they stop other plants and animals from thriving. Answer the following questions in your science journal. What is the name, color, and size of the species? How did it arrive in your country? How does it spread? In your journal, mark on a world map where the species came from. Draw a picture of the species and add as many details as you can.

PROJECT!

A SALTY SEA

People have harvested salt from the sea for hundreds of years. Let's see how this process works.

SUPPLIES

* ✳ science journal and pencil
* ✳ warm water
* ✳ 3 saucers
* ✳ table salt
* ✳ teaspoon measure
* ✳ popsicle stick

1 Start a scientific method worksheet in your science journal and write down a prediction. How long do you think it will take for the water to evaporate completely?

2 Pour warm water into a saucer. Add a teaspoon of salt at a time to the water and stir it with a popsicle stick. Stop when the salt no longer dissolves.

3 Place the saucer in a sunny spot.

4 For the next few days, observe the saucer and write down your observations in your science journal. Add diagrams to show what you are seeing.

5 Compare your results with your prediction.

WORDS TO KNOW

dissolve: to mix with a liquid and become part of the liquid.

mine: to dig something out of the ground.

24

IT'S ALL MINE!

The ocean floor has many valuable mineral deposits, including copper, manganese, cobalt, and lithium. These minerals are used in many different products, including batteries, computers, and construction materials. However, these minerals have not yet been mined from the ocean floor. Engineers are working to develop technology to make this possible. But more studies must also be done to learn how taking deep-sea minerals will impact the ocean.

THINK ABOUT IT! Where did the water go? How could you make the water evaporate more quickly? Write down your ideas in your science journal.

TRY THIS! Does stirring the salt change the results? Fill three saucers with warm water and table salt. Stir the salt mixture in one saucer in circles. Trace the letter S with the stick in another. Leave one mixture unstirred. Leave the saucers for a few days. What happens? Do you notice any differences?

CHAPTER 2

EXTRAORDINARY EXPLORATION

Imagine waking up in the middle of the ocean. You lean
over the side of your rubber dingy. Miles of water are
all around you. How will you find your way home?

Today, sailors use a tool called GPS. GPS stands for Global
Positioning System. It's the same system that people use on
their cell phones or in their cars. Signals from GPS satellites
tell sailors what their
longitude, latitude, and
speed are to help them
to reach their destination
safely.

? INVESTIGATE!

What methods did sailors
use in the past to find their
way on the open ocean?

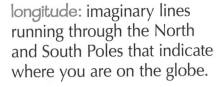

Let's look at how people explored the oceans before GPS!

EARLY OCEAN EXPLORERS

The ancient Phoenicians lived in present-day Lebanon and Syria. At the height of their civilization (1600–1200 BCE), they sailed all around the Mediterranean to trade goods with other cultures. The Phoenicians even sailed as far as the Atlantic coast of Africa.

Phoenician sailors used landmarks by the coast to know where they were. They also used the sun, moon, and stars to navigate. To sail by the stars, Phoenician sailors learned to find the North Star to figure out their position.

longitude: imaginary lines running through the North and South Poles that indicate where you are on the globe.

latitude: imaginary lines around the earth that measure a position north or south of the equator.

civilization: a community of people that is advanced in art, science, and government.

culture: a group of people who share beliefs and a way of life.

navigate: to find your way from one place to another.

WORDS TO KNOW

Early Polynesian sailors made maps based on wave patterns and currents. Have you ever tossed a rock into a lake and seen the water ripple? Polynesians noticed that near islands, waves behaved in much the same way.

compass: a device that uses a magnet to show which direction is north.

naturalist: a person who studies nature.

crustacean: a type of animal, such as a crab or lobster, that lives mainly in water. It has several pairs of legs and its body is made up of sections covered in a hard outer shell.

WORDS TO KNOW

Sailors used their knowledge of the ocean and the islands to make maps or stick charts that used shells, sticks, and coconut fibers to show where islands and ocean currents could be found. Before a journey, sailors memorized their stick chart by heart. Why do you think they did this instead of taking it with them?

The ancient Chinese are also known for their navigation tools. They made the first magnetic compass, known as a wet compass. Sailors put a magnetic needle in a stone bowl of water. The needle turned to point in the north-south directions. Sailors used this information to determine other directions.

EARLY SCIENTIFIC EXPLORATIONS

As people made technological advances in shipbuilding and tools for navigation, they explored further.

In 1831, a British scientist named Charles Darwin (1809–1882) sailed on a ship called the *HMS Beagle* on a scientific journey around the world. Darwin joined the ship's crew as the chief naturalist. He drew pictures of shells, plants, and crustaceans. Darwin's ideas changed how scientists studied the natural world.

WHY DID CHRISTOPHER COLUMBUS CROSS THE OCEAN?

To get to the other tide.

In 1872, a ship built specifically for ocean research left Great Britain. It was called the *HMS Challenger*. A team of scientists gathered samples from the ocean using a system of ropes attached to glass bottles. They used thermometers to record ocean temperatures. They also mapped areas of the seafloor by measuring depth.

The *HMS Challenger* sailed to 362 different locations during four years. Scientists explored areas at the southernmost tip of Africa, the Indian Ocean, and New Zealand. They recorded 4,700 new species, including the giant Pacific octopus. This species of octopus grows larger than any other in the world. The largest giant Pacific octopus ever discovered weighed more than 400 pounds!

Are you interested in what Darwin's marine samples looked like? **Find out at the website for the National History Museum in London.**

KEYWORD PROMPTS

National History Museum London 🔍

MODERN EXPLORERS

By the twentieth century, scientists could explore underwater for longer periods of time. For example, oceanographers Jacques Cousteau (1910–1997) and Émile Gagnan (1900–1979) invented the scuba tank in 1943. In this early version, divers used a mouthpiece connected to a tank of air. The tank allowed them to swim and breathe underwater.

In 1977, three marine scientists, including Robert Ballard (1942–) and J.F. Grassle (1939–), dove 8,000 feet below

the ocean surface in a mini submarine called a submersible. They made an unexpected discovery. They saw jets of black water gushing from chimney-like rocks and water seeping through cracks on the ocean floor. These cracks are known as hydrothermal vents.

A HYDROTHERMAL VENT
CREDIT: NOAA, P. RONA

DID YOU KNOW?

Giant squids have lidless eyes. Some grow as large as beach balls.

dead reckoning: a method of determining a ship's position by using a previously determined position and the distance traveled.

WORDS ⏃ KNOW

Amazingly, the scientists found an ecosystem around these vents. Animals included ghostly white tube worms, lava rocks dotted with blind white crabs, and giant clams.

TUBE WORMS
CREDIT: NOAA OKEANOS EXPLORER PROGRAM, GALAPAGOS RIFT EXPEDITION 2011

THEN & NOW

THEN: Early navigators charted a ship's position based on its previous location and speed. This method is called dead reckoning.

NOW: Ocean navigators rely on GPS to tell them where they are and where they are going.

SYLVIA EARLE

Sylvia Earle (1935–) is a marine scientist who has been diving since she was 17 years old. In 1979, her research took her to Oahu, Hawaii. In order to dive deep under the surface of the ocean, she had to wear a special diving suit that looked like armor. The suit served an important purpose—it kept Earle from being crushed by the weight of the water above. Earle dove 1,250 feet deep, setting a world record. She watched as fish lit up the darkness around her by using special chemicals in their bodies. She saw plants that spit out rings of blue light. Earle went on to lead more than 70 scientific expeditions. She has dived in waters off Cuba, China, and the Galapagos Islands.

On March 26, 2012, movie director and underwater explorer James Cameron (1954–) descended 7 miles below the surface in the *Deepsea Challenger* submersible. Cameron spent three hours in the deepest point on Earth—the Mariana Trench. The Mariana Trench is 38,400 feet below the surface of the Pacific Ocean.

DID YOU KNOW?

Temperatures in underwater volcanoes can reach 650 degrees Fahrenheit. That's hot enough to melt lead.

Humans have a strong connection with the ocean, but what about the other creatures that live there and need the ocean to survive? We'll learn about the animals of the ocean in the next chapter!

? CONSIDER AND DISCUSS

It's time to consider and discuss: What methods did sailors use in the past to find their way on the open ocean?

PROJECT!

STICK CHART

SUPPLIES

* science journal and pencil
* push pins
* Styrofoam tray (shoebox lid)
* small shells
* white glue or tape
* ball of string

This activity shows you how Polynesian sailors created sailing charts based on their knowledge of ocean waves and currents. You can see some Polynesian stick charts at this website.

KEYWORD PROMPTS

Polynesian stick chart 🔍

Things to Know

- Horizontal and vertical sticks act as supports.

- Diagonal and curved sticks represent waves.

- Small shells represent islands.

1 In your science journal, write the four basic directions on a page. Think about where the islands are first and how the water moves near land. Next, sketch your map.

2 Copy your sketch onto the Styrofoam with the pencil. Glue or tape the shells to the Styrofoam to show where the islands are.

3 Use the push pins to plot your map. Tie and loop the string from pin to pin until you complete your map.

TRY THIS! Share your map with friends. Ask them if they can find the islands, waves, and open ocean. What would the world be like with no ocean currents?

PROJECT!

DIVING BELL

SUPPLIES

* science journal and pencil
* small mixing bowl
* water
* clear drinking glass
* spoon
* piece of clay
* piece of tissue paper

Before scuba tanks were invented, people used a hollow container called a diving bell to explore underwater. They put this container filled with air over their heads. By the 1700s, a hose connected the bell to a diver wearing a glass helmet like a fishbowl. Learn how a diving bell works in this activity.

1 Start a scientific method worksheet in your science journal and write down a prediction. What will happen to the paper when you put the glass in the water?

2 Fill the bowl with tap water until it is three-quarters full.

3 Push a piece of clay to the bottom of the glass with the spoon.

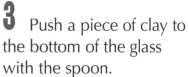

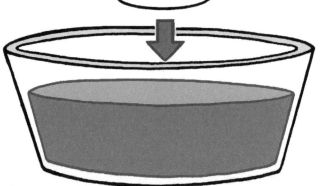

4 Scrunch up the tissue paper into a ball and stick it to the clay with the spoon.

5 Test your prediction. Invert the glass and lower it to the bottom of the bowl. Write down your observations in your journal.

OCEAN EXPLORATION

In the eighteenth century, Captain James Cook (1728–1779), an explorer from England, made many daring voyages. He used his experiences to map large areas of the globe. In 1776, Captain Cook made a journey to find a sea route across the Arctic. Called the Northwest Passage, it would link the Atlantic and Pacific Oceans. On this incredible journey, he wrote of ice walls more than one story high. Though he never found the passage, scientists still study Captain Cook's journals. His writings help them understand how Arctic sea ice has changed.

THINK ABOUT IT! What is happening to the water around the glass? What keeps the water from entering the glass?

TRY THIS! A diving bell was lowered into the ocean with a **simple machine** called a **pulley**. Use a small plastic container, string, and a removable press-on hook to create a pulley. Put the hook on a wall about knee height. Cut a long piece of thread. Tie the thread to the container and loop the string over the hook. In which direction do you need to pull to raise or lower the container?

MEASURING SCALE

SUPPLIES

* ball of yarn
* ruler
* scissors
* eraser
* lint roller sheet (or masking tape)
* science journal and pencil

Before the modern technology of navigation, sailors used a long piece of rope marked with measurements and a heavy weight at the bottom to measure the depth at sea. This tool is called a lead line. To see how it works, try this activity.

1 Sailors measure depth in fathoms. A fathom is roughly 6 feet. You can use a smaller scale, such as a foot or a yard, to take measurements around your home.

2 Take the ball of yarn and ruler and knot the string at your chosen unit of measure. Continue this step until you have made about 20 measured knots. Cut off the excess yarn.

3 To copy dropping a lead line into the ocean, tie a small weight, such as an eraser, to the bottom of the string. Stand on a chair and drop your line from crouching, kneeling, and standing positions. Write down the measurements in your science journal.

TRY THIS! Lead lines were also used to take samples from the ocean floor. Sailors attached a lump of fat to the bottom of the line. The fat picked up fragments on the ocean floor. Sailors used this knowledge to figure out where they were on the ocean. Sand, for example, told a sailor that they were getting closer to shore. Attach a piece of two-sided tape to your eraser. Reel your line in and out. What did your samples tell you about the different rooms in your house?

WORDS TO KNOW

fathom: a measurement of about 6 feet.

FIND NORTH

SUPPLIES

* saucer
* water
* sewing needle
* magnet
* plastic bottle cap
* clear tape
* science journal and pencil
* magnetic compass or phone app

Once navigators knew where north was, they could figure out the other directions. To see how a compass works, try this.

1 Fill the saucer with water and set it to one side.

2 Rub the needle on the magnet in one direction to magnetize it. Use long strokes for a few seconds or at least 20 strokes.

3 Tape the needle onto the bottle cap with clear tape.

4 Place the bottle cap, needle side up, in the saucer of water. What happens? Write down your observations.

5 Use the store-bought compass or phone app to see if your needle is pointing north.

TRY THIS! Use your compass to figure out which direction your home faces. Next, use your compass to figure out the direction to your school, a friend's home, or the nearest grocery store. Write down the locations and the directions in your science journal. Can a friend read your directions and understand them?

CHAPTER 3

CREATURES OF THE DEEP

What lives in the ocean? Oceanographers and marine biologists are interested in answering that question. These scientists have discovered more than 1 million species of plants and animals living in different ocean habitats.

Some animals live along the coastline. Other animals make their home among reefs or at the bottom of the ocean, where light can't reach them. New species are being discovered every year. Scientists believe that the number of known plants and animals in the ocean could rise to 9 million.

 INVESTIGATE!

How do scientists determine ocean zones?

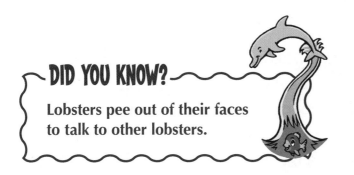

DID YOU KNOW?

Lobsters pee out of their faces to talk to other lobsters.

The ocean is divided into three major layers called zones. Each zone receives a different amount of sunlight. Water near the surface is bright and warm. The deep ocean is cold and pitch black. Let's look at the different zones.

habitat: an area where certain plants and animals live together.

reef: an underwater structure made of corals, sand, and rock.

zone: an area of the ocean based on depth.

sunlight zone: an area of the ocean from the surface to where light doesn't reach, usually about 600 feet below.

predator: an animal that hunts other animals for food.

SUNLIGHT ZONE

WORDS ᴛᴏ KNOW

The sunlight zone is closest to the surface. It's where you swim. As much as 90 percent of all marine life lives in the sunlight

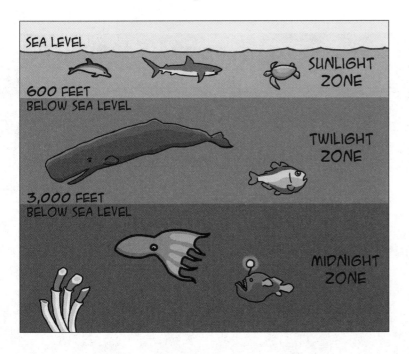

SEA LEVEL

SUNLIGHT ZONE

600 FEET BELOW SEA LEVEL

TWILIGHT ZONE

3,000 FEET BELOW SEA LEVEL

MIDNIGHT ZONE

zone. Sea lions live and feed in the sunlight zone of the Pacific and Indian Oceans. Depending on the ocean, they eat lobsters, crabs, sea birds, and octopuses. Sea lions must always be on the lookout for the biggest predators— sharks.

39

One of the larger fish that live in the sunlight zone is the hammerhead shark. Some species of hammerheads can reach up to 20 feet in length. The hammerhead has a flat head, which acts like a giant fly swatter, trapping prey on the seafloor.

The largest animal to ever live on Earth lives in the sunlight zone. It's the blue whale. The blue whale is as long as three school buses. Despite its huge size, the blue whale eats tiny, shrimp-like animals called krill. A blue whale isn't satisfied with a single krill. The whale's appetite is enormous. It eats millions of krill each day.

DID YOU KNOW?

Sharks never run out of teeth because they constantly make new ones. Some types of sharks lose more than 50,000 teeth in their lifetime.

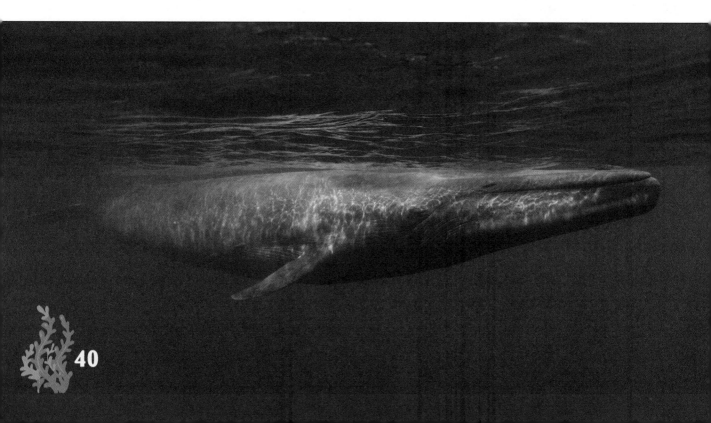

TWILIGHT ZONE

The twilight zone begins at about 600 feet beneath the surface. Not enough sunlight means few plants live in this zone. Fewer animals also live there. Animals that live in this zone have adapted to live with less light. Some have large eyes to help them see more clearly. Other animals survive in this zone by changing their color or the shape of their body to blend into their surroundings.

twilight zone: a dim area of the ocean that begins at about 600 feet below the surface.

adapt: to make changes to better survive in an environment.

camouflage: colors or patterns that animals use to blend in with their environment.

WORDS TO KNOW

The Japetella heathi octopus lives in the twilight zone. This octopus has see-through skin and can camouflage itself by changing the color of its skin to red!

The hatchet fish has also evolved to live in the twilight zone. It has large eyes that help it spot prey. One type of hatchet fish has bulging eyes that face upward. These eyes help the fish spot potential prey as it swims to the ocean surface to feed. Plus, the belly and tail of the hatchet fish produce light! When predators see the light, they mistake it for sunshine and leave it alone.

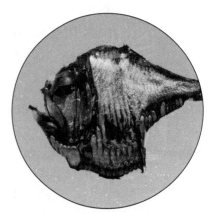

A HATCHET FISH
CREDIT: NOAA (CC BY 2.0)

PS You can watch a short movie about the hatchet fish at this website.

KEYWORD PROMPTS

bioluminescence Blue Planet BBC Earth

midnight zone: an area of the ocean between 3,000 feet below the surface and the seafloor.

Challenger Deep: the deepest known point in the earth's seabed at the bottom of the Mariana Trench in the Pacific Ocean.

marine snow: what falls to the ocean floor when marine animals die or excrete waste.

WORDS TO KNOW

MIDNIGHT ZONE

Get ready to plunge into complete darkness! The midnight zone is so deep that sunlight cannot reach it. This zone begins at around 3,000 feet below the surface. It's the biggest habitat on Earth. It is also one of the biggest mysteries on our planet. Only three people have ever been to its deepest point—the Challenger Deep at the bottom of the Mariana Trench.

Scientists once thought that nothing could live in this deep and dark region. They thought that all life needed to harness energy from the sun to live. In 1977, scientists learned that they were wrong. Many animals live in the deepest trenches of the oceans, including tube worms and giant clams.

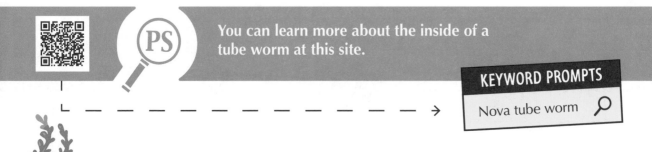

WHAT DO WHALES EAT?

Fish and ships.

Other creatures in the midnight zone feed on the remains of dead ocean plants and animals that sink from the surface, called marine snow. Marine snow is an important part of the vampire squid's diet.

PS You can learn more about the inside of a tube worm at this site.

KEYWORD PROMPTS

Nova tube worm

invertebrate: an animal without a backbone.

bacteria: tiny organisms found in animals, plants, soil, and water.

WORDS to KNOW

THEN: Long ago, sailors thought the giant squid was a sea monster.

NOW: The giant squid is known as the largest invertebrate on Earth.

The vampire squid shoots through the water with webbing like Count Dracula's cape! The webbing is strung between its eight arms. The squid uses the webbing to catch marine snow. The name makes it sound like a monster from a scary movie, but you wouldn't run away from a vampire squid screaming. It's just 12 inches long!

Many species of anglerfish also use light to catch prey. The deep-sea anglerfish has a built-in fishing rod on top of its head—a fin with a lure that lights up. The light is produced by millions of bacteria.

A 1910 DRAWING OF THE VAMPIRE SQUID BY CARL CHUN

To catch prey, the anglerfish wiggles the lure to look like a shrimp or a worm. Smaller fish can't help but swim closer to see what the light is. Could it be something tasty? The anglerfish then opens its large mouth and—snap! Another delicious meal is caught.

The ocean is full of incredible creatures! In the next chapter, we'll look plants that provide food, shelter, and even oxygen to animals and humans.

CONSIDER AND DISCUSS

It's time to consider and discuss: How do scientists determine ocean zones?

OCEAN ZONES

Make a model of the three major ocean zones with your favorite marine animals.

1 Wrap the sheet of computer paper around the jar. Mark the excess paper with the pencil. Remove the paper, use the ruler to draw a line at this mark, and cut off the excess.

2 Use the ruler to divide the paper into three horizontal sections.

3 Using the information in this chapter, fill in the three ocean zones with pictures of animals that live in each zone. You can also research to find more animals to add to each zone.

4 Wrap the paper around the jar with the pictures facing inward. Secure the paper with tape.

5 Pour the corn syrup into the jar—just to the top edge of the midnight zone on your paper. Add a few drops of blue and red coloring to make it purple. Stir with the spoon.

6 In the jug, mix water with one drop of blue food coloring. Slowly pour this mixture over the corn syrup until you reach the top of the twilight zone.

SUPPLIES

* large mason jar with lid
* sheet of computer paper
* ruler
* pencil
* scissors
* pencil crayons, markers, stickers,
* clear tape
* corn syrup
* blue and red food coloring
* 2 spoons
* jug
* water
* vegetable oil

WORDS TO KNOW

horizontal: straight across from side to side.

44

7 Slowly add the vegetable oil until it reaches the top of the sunlight zone.

8 Look into the top of the jar to see the ocean zones and the animals that live in them.

DID YOU KNOW?

A team of engineers worked to build the *Deepsea Challenger* submarine for more than seven years. The submarine had to be able to withstand the crushing pressure in the trench. This pressure is about 1,000 times greater than the pressure on the earth's surface.

THINK ABOUT IT!
Almost 90 percent of all marine life lives in the sunlight zone. Why do you think this is? In this chapter, you read of animals that moved between ocean zones. Why did they do this?

SEND SECRET MESSAGES

SUPPLIES

* science journal and pencil
* 2 glowsticks

Bioluminescent **animals use light to send messages. Try this activity to send a message with light.**

1 First, write one word in your science journal. Translate this word into Morse code using dots and dashes. You can find a Morse code translator at this website.

KEYWORD PROMPTS

Morse code convert 🔍

2 Dim the lights in a room. Use the glowstick to send this word. Hint: Remember to pause between each letter.

3 Next, think of a longer message to send and translate it into Morse code.

> **DID YOU KNOW?**
>
> **The dwarf lantern shark is the smallest shark in the world. It could fit in your hand.**

4 Use the glowstick to send the message to a friend. Can your friend figure out the message? Your friend may want to write the flashes down on a piece of paper.

5 Have your friend send a message back to you.

TRY THIS! Create your own secret code. Instead of light, what could you use?

WORDS ᴛᴏ **KNOW**

bioluminescent: describes an organism that produces its own light.

Morse code: a code in which letters are represented by combinations of dots and dashes, or long and short signals of light or sound.

JETS OF THE OCEAN

SUPPLIES

* ✳ science journal and pencil
* ✳ 10 feet of string
* ✳ straw
* ✳ a disposable latex glove or balloon
* ✳ masking tape

Squids belong to a group of creatures called cephalopods. **Cephalopods fill their bodies with water and let it out quickly to move through the ocean. Try this activity to see how this works.**

1 Make a scientific method worksheet in your science journal. Predict which way the balloon will move when you let it go.

2 Tie one end of the string to a doorknob. Thread the string through a straw and attach the other end to a table leg about 8 feet away.

3 Blow into the disposable glove to fill it up and pinch the end. Tape one of the fingers of the glove to the straw with the pinched end facing away from the door.

4 Release the glove and watch what happens. Compare your results with your prediction. How far did your squid travel? What would happen if you filled the glove with less or more air? Try this and see.

TRY THIS! Many fish, including the seahorse, have swim bladders. The seahorse fills its swim bladder with air to move upward and releases air to go down. To see how this works, fill a bowl with water. Next, blow up a balloon, push it to the bottom of the bowl, and release it. It pops back up because air is lighter than water.

WORDS TO KNOW

cephalopod: a class of mollusks, including the squid and octopus, characterized by their ability to fill their bodies with water and quickly let it out in order to move.

PROJECT!

VOLCANO MODEL

Learn how underwater volcanoes work in this experiment.

> **Caution:** Ask an adult help you with the hot water.

1 Start a scientific method worksheet in your science journal.

2 Fill one jug with water to the three-quarter-cup line. Let the water sit until it is room temperature.

3 Attach one chopstick to each side of the small jar by wrapping a piece of masking tape around the circumference of the bottle. You will use the chopsticks to raise and lower the bottle.

4 Fill the second jug with hot water until it hits the half-cup line. The water doesn't need to boil.

5 Add a few drops of red food coloring to the hot water and stir. Fill the small food jar to the rim with the red water.

DID YOU KNOW?

The material that erupts from underwater volcanoes is called magma. It flows to the bottom of the ocean to become new ocean floor. The material can build up to create new islands!

WORDS TO KNOW

circumference: the distance around the edge of a circle.

magma: hot, flowing rock below the surface of the earth.

dense: when something is tightly packed in its space.

48

6 Using the chopsticks, lower the bottle to the bottom of the jug with room temperature water. Do not let go.

7 What happens? Write down your observations on your scientific method worksheet and add pictures.

WHAT IS HAPPENING? Hot water is less **dense** than cold water, so it rises to the top. In a volcano, the magma rises because it is less dense than the rock around it.

TRY THIS! Repeat this experiment with different temperatures of water. Write down each of your results in your science journal.

CHAPTER 4

OCEAN PLANTS

• • • • • • • • • • • • • • • • •

**Have you ever gone swimming in the ocean?
Did you feel seaweed wrapping itself around
your ankles? The ocean is full of plant life!**

• •

Ocean plants are an important source of food for marine
animals, including snails, sea urchins, and turtles. The leafy
parts of plants help animals hide from predators that want to
eat them. Humans rely on
ocean plants, too. They are
a source of oxygen in our
atmosphere.

? INVESTIGATE!

Which ocean zone do most
plants live in and why?

Most ocean plants grow in the sunlight zone. They need the sun to make energy.

Seagrasses and algae are the two major types of marine plants. Seagrasses have roots and stems. Algae don't have roots, so they float on the ocean surface or cling to surfaces such as rocks. There are more than 25,000 types of marine algae. Algae include seaweed, kelp, and phytoplankton.

oxygen: a gas in the air that animals and humans need to breathe to stay alive.

phytoplankton: tiny organisms that are at the base of ocean food chains.

photosynthesis: the process plants use to turn sunlight, carbon dioxide, and water into food.

WORDS ⊙ KNOW

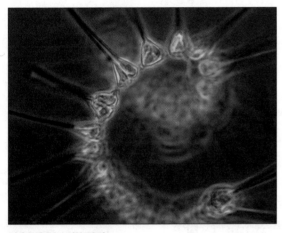

PHYTOPLANKTON
CREDIT: NOAA

PHYTOPLANKTON

Take three deep breaths. Tiny ocean plants called phytoplankton made two of those breaths possible! Phytoplankton produce more of the world's oxygen than tropical rainforests. They produce oxygen through a process called photosynthesis.

DID YOU KNOW?

Prochlorococcus is one of the tiniest phytoplankton. It's so small that a teaspoon of water holds one million of them. This tiny plant is responsible for supplying 10 percent of the oxygen in the atmosphere.

51

absorb: to soak up.

carbon dioxide: a gas formed by the burning of fossil fuels, the rotting of plants and animals, and the breathing out of animals or humans.

nutrients: substances in food, water, and soil that living things need to live and grow.

food chain: a community of animals and plants where each is eaten by another higher up in the chain.

WORDS ⊕ KNOW

During this process, phytoplankton absorb carbon dioxide from the atmosphere. They also take nutrients from the water. Using sunlight, the plants turn the carbon dioxide into sugar and release oxygen.

Phytoplankton are also important because they are at the base of the marine food chain. Sardines, anchovies, herrings, and other small fish feed on phytoplankton. These small fish are then eaten by larger predators, such as halibut, salmon, and barracudas.

KELP FORESTS

After a powerful storm, you may see strands of lettuce-like plants on the beach. These plants are called kelp. Kelp is a type of algae. Some types of kelp are visible only with a microscope, but others are much larger. One species of kelp can grow up to 16 stories tall! It's called giant kelp. Giant kelp form towering forests of green in the ocean. The plants can grow up to 12 inches a day!

WHERE DOES SEAWEED LOOK FOR WORK?

In the kelp wanted section.

Watch a live video of the kelp forest at Channel Islands National Park.

KEYWORD PROMPTS

explore livecam Anacapa ocean

Kelp grows in shallow waters near the shore. It has a long, smooth stalk called a stipe. The flexible stipe allows kelp to sway with the waves. Kelp does not have roots, but it does have a holdfast, which anchors the plant to rocks.

When many kelp plants grow together, they form a leafy kelp forest. Kelp forests can be found off the coasts of Europe, Africa, Australia, and North and South America. Kelp forests are even in the freezing waters of the Arctic. In North America, the largest kelp forests are off the Pacific Coast.

FORESTS OF THE SEA

Have you ever been in a bay or a lagoon along the coast? If so, perhaps you saw what looked like a meadow beneath the water. This is actually a flowering plant called seagrass. Scientists think that seagrass has been around for 100 million years.

Seagrass beds are important habitats for many species of fish, crustaceans, and mammals. One acre of seagrass supports up to 40,000 fish and 50 million small invertebrates, such as snails.

53

Seagrass leaves also trap pollution. They soak up carbon dioxide, which can help us fight climate change.

You've seen how animals and plants live together in the ocean and rely on each other to stay alive. What happens when this balance is upset by weather, climate, or natural disaster? We'll find out in the next chapter.

?

CONSIDER AND DISCUSS

It's time to consider and discuss: Which ocean zone do most plants live in and why?

SEAGRASS

Seagrass grows in shallow waters because the plant needs sunlight to produce energy and food. More than 60 species of seagrass grow in the world. Seagrass even grows under Arctic sea ice. The only continent in the world where seagrass does not grow is Antarctica.

PS Learn more about seagrass by watching this video.

KEYWORD PROMPTS

PBS seagrass mangroves

GIANT KELP MODEL

Scientists often build models to help them visualize how something happens. You can learn how seagrass plants have adapted to life in the ocean by building models. Ask an adult for help researching giant kelp at the library and on the internet.

1 When researching images of giant kelp, sketch the plant in your science journal. Your pictures should include the stipe, blades, and gas-filled floats that allow the entire plant to float.

2 From the supplies list above, build two models to test. Think about how you will make the stipe sturdy. Think about the size and shape of the blades.

3 After you build your models, write a prediction in your science journal. Which model do you think will be the sturdiest and why?

4 Test one model at a time. Secure the model to a flat surface such as a table. Take the paper plate and quickly fan the air in front of the model. The breeze represents the wind and ocean currents. Did the stipe bend? Did the size of the blades or shape make a difference in how your models moved? What does this tell you about kelp?

TRY THIS! Based on your data, build one more model and test it. Did your results change? If so, how?

WORDS TO KNOW

float: the little bubble on kelp filled with gas that helps keep the kelp afloat.

PROJECT!

KELP STRENGTH

Kelp must be strong and flexible to survive being tossed back and forth by ocean currents. This experiment shows you the strength of kelp.

1 Start a scientific method worksheet in your science journal. Write a prediction about how much water the kelp will be able to hold before it breaks.

2 Fill the mixing bowl three-quarters full of water. Place the dried kelp in the water until it is soft.

3 Take a piece of kelp from the bowl and drape it over a faucet with a long neck.

4 Cut the kitchen sponge in half. Sandwich the sponge between the kelp ends and hold it in place with the binder clip.

5 Cut two short pieces of string. Push the strings through the prongs of the binder clip. Then, tape the ends to the container to make a handle.

SUPPLIES

* science journal and pencil
* 2 to 4 dried kelp or kombu sheets from a specialty grocery store or online
* mixing bowl
* kitchen sponge
* extra-large binder clip
* large clean yogurt-sized container
* string
* scissors
* masking tape
* measuring jug
* water
* 2 daylily leaves

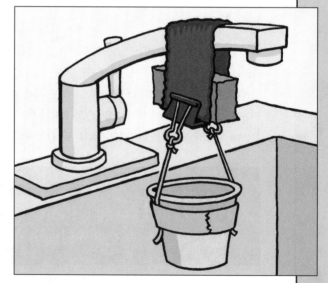

BEAUTIFUL KELP

The Channel Islands National Park and Marine Sanctuary off the coast of California contains almost a third of California's kelp forests. Many different animals shelter in these kelp forests. Brightly colored anemones, spiny sea urchins, and orange sunflower sea stars live here. The sunflower sea star is the largest species of sea star in the forest. Some grow up to 39 inches from tip to tip!

6 Do not turn on the tap to fill the container. Slowly pour water from the jug into the container. Stop when the kelp breaks.

7 Write down your observations in your journal. Compare your results with your prediction.

TRY THIS! Repeat the experiment above with a daylily leaf. Write down your observations. Were your results different? If so, how and why do you think this was?

THINK ABOUT IT! How are the structures of the kelp and the daylily leaf similar or different? Write your answer and draw pictures in your journal. Do you think your results would be different if you used another type of land plant?

LET'S BREATHE

Most of the air we breathe comes from ocean plants. To learn how many of your breaths come from the ocean, try this activity.

1 Turn on some ocean music at a low level. Sit quietly with your back against a wall and stretch out your legs in front of you. Place one hand on your chest. You will need to take deep breaths. Imagine that breath beginning at your toes and traveling all the way up to the top of your head. Then, slowly exhale all the air. Now, ask an adult to set the timer to one minute.

2 Count how many breaths you take in that minute. Write the number down in your journal. Repeat this two or three more times. Write down your results.

DID YOU KNOW?

The oxygen that you breathe comes from these sources:
70 percent marine plants,
28 percent rainforests,
2 percent other sources

3 Two in every three breaths is possible because of the ocean. Take your number of breaths, divide it by three, then multiply this by two to determine how many breaths were from the ocean. Write this number down in your journal.

TRY THIS!

Create a circle graph to show the sources of the earth's oxygen. You'll need to use the information highlighted above. Use a pencil compass to make a circle. The entire circle represents 100 percent. Use the oxygen data above to divide your circle. Color in each area and label. What other types of graphs could you make to show this information?

PLANTS CREATE OXYGEN

Sunlight affects how plants grow. This experiment will help you understand the importance of sunlight to plants.

SUPPLIES

* science journal and pencil
* 1 live plant (large leaves are easier to work with)
* foil

Caution: Ask an adult for permission to use the plant.

1 Create a scientific method worksheet in your science journal. Then, predict what will happen to the section of leaf covered in foil.

2 Take your plant and cover one of the leaves with foil. Pinch the edges to hold the foil in place.

3 Place the plant in a sunny spot and wait one week. After a week, remove the foil and record your results. You should see a difference between the covered leaf and the leaves that were not covered.

THINK ABOUT IT!

What does your experiment tell you about why most marine plants grow in the sunlight zone?

TRY THIS!
Place a green leaf in a clear glass of water and put it in the sunlight for an hour. You should see tiny bubbles forming on the leaf and on the glass. Those bubbles are oxygen.

Phytoplankton are major producers of oxygen. **Learn more about the importance of phytoplankton at this website.**

KEYWORD PROMPTS

Nat Geo plankton revealed 🔍

SEAWEED ROLLS

You can make your own seaweed rolls. You may need an adult to help you with this recipe.

1 Cut open the avocado and scoop out the pulp into the bowl. Mash the avocado to your liking. You can also cut it into long slices if you'd prefer. Season with salt.

2 Place one sheet of nori on a dry cutting board and spread the avocado evenly over it. Leave a thumbprint's worth of space at the end.

3 Use the vegetable peeler to slice the cucumber into long pieces. You need to slice enough to cover the avocado mixture. Pat any excess moisture in the cucumber out with the paper towel. Place the cucumber over the avocado.

SUPPLIES

* ✳ ripe avocado
* ✳ knife
* ✳ fork
* ✳ small bowl
* ✳ salt
* ✳ sheet of nori (dried seaweed)
* ✳ seedless cucumber
* ✳ vegetable peeler
* ✳ paper towel
* ✳ carrot
* ✳ sesame seeds

THEN & NOW

THEN: Seaweed has been an important food in Japan for centuries.

NOW: As many as 70,000 fishermen in Japan grow seaweed for the food industry.

4 Use the vegetable peeler to slice a few pieces of carrot and place on top of the cucumber. Sprinkle with sesame seeds.

5 Roll the nori and dab the ends with water to make them stick together. Slice your roll in half and enjoy.

TRY THIS! Have fun with this recipe. What other vegetables could you add to your roll? Do you think banana, nut butter, peanut butter, or cream cheese would work? Try and see.

USEFUL SEAGRASS

Seagrasses have been an important natural resource for thousands of years. In parts of England, seagrass was once used instead of straw to cover roofs. Dried seagrass was stuffed into pillows and chairs. In the Netherlands, people wanted to make their dikes stronger to hold back ocean waters. Can you guess what they used? Seagrass! The roots of the seagrass kept the sand in place.

WORDS TO KNOW

dike: a long earthen wall built to prevent flooding.

CHAPTER 5

OCEANS, WEATHER, AND CLIMATE

A sudden crack of thunder is followed by a burst of rain! The raindrops tickling your nose once floated in clouds. They rushed over waterfalls. They rolled onto beaches. They spent time frozen in a glacier. How is this possible? Because Earth's water is always on the move in the water cycle.

The ocean has a big role in the water cycle because most of the earth's water is held here. The ocean also has a big influence on weather and climate. What does this mean? Let's find out more.

 INVESTIGATE!

Why is the ocean an important part of the earth's weather and climate?

THE WATER CYCLE

It's Monday morning and you're going to school. The sun is shining brightly. You feel warm enough to wear shorts and a T-shirt.

Heat from the sun also warms up the ocean. As ocean water heats up, it changes form. Through evaporation, the liquid water changes into a gas, called water vapor. The water vapor rises into the air.

> **water cycle:** the continuous movement of water from the earth to the clouds and back again.
>
> **water vapor:** the gas form of water.
>
> **WORDS TO KNOW**

DUCKS ON THE MOVE

In 1992, the cargo ship *Ever Laurel* hit a strong storm as it sailed from China to North America. A container tumbled overboard and out spilled about 28,000 rubber ducks, blue turtles, and green frogs. The toys became known as the Friendly Floatees, and this was the beginning of their ocean adventure. An oceanographer named Curt Ebbesmeyer (1943–) wanted to see where these toys would end up. During the next few years, the toys traveled 17,000 miles. Some washed up on the coasts of Hawaii, Australia, and South America. Other toys spent years frozen in an Arctic ice pack. The toys also made their way to beaches in Scotland, Newfoundland, and Tacoma, Washington. Because of ocean currents, the toys were able to travel nearly all the way around the world.

PS You can read a National Public Radio interview with a journalist who tracked the Friendly Floatees.

KEYWORD PROMPTS

NPR moby duck

> **condensation:** the process of a gas cooling down and changing into a liquid.
>
> **rotation:** a turn all the way around.

WORDS TO KNOW

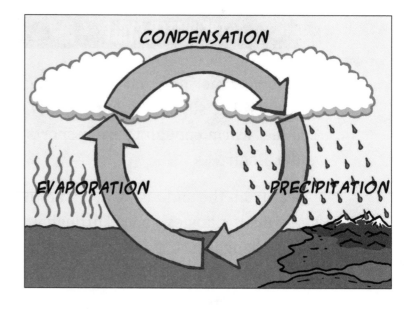

As the water vapor rises, it cools and turns into clouds. This is called condensation. Water droplets in the clouds grow so large that they become too heavy to stay in the air. They fall back to the earth as rain or snow.

And soon, this happens all over again. Once on land, water eventually flows into the ocean and other bodies of water and evaporates. The cycle keeps going, forever repeating itself.

SURFACE CURRENTS

Oceans have two types of currents. Surface currents move water around the top of the ocean. Deep ocean currents move water far below the surface. Surface currents are driven by wind and the earth's spin, or rotation.

Learn more about the water cycle at this website.

KEYWORD PROMPTS

NASA earth water cycle

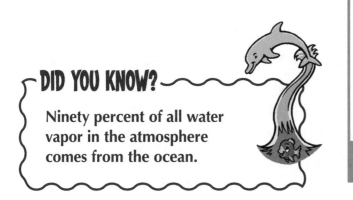

DID YOU KNOW?

Ninety percent of all water vapor in the atmosphere comes from the ocean.

clockwise: the direction that follows the hands of a clock.

counterclockwise: the direction that goes opposite to the hands of a clock.

WORDS TO KNOW

As the earth spins, it also moves around the sun. The earth's spin causes the air in the Northern Hemisphere to move to the right. The air pulls on the ocean, which means ocean currents north of the equator move to the right, too. They flow clockwise. The wind in the Southern Hemisphere moves to the left. So, currents south of the equator curve left. They flow counterclockwise.

Ocean currents affect weather and climate on land by spreading heat over the earth's surface. The Gulf Stream is the largest surface current in the

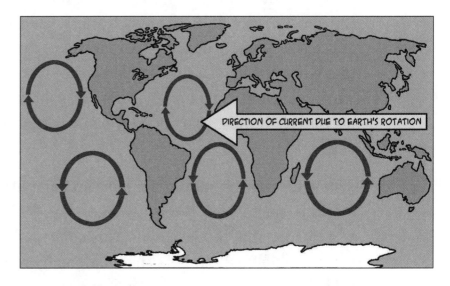

DIRECTION OF CURRENT DUE TO EARTH'S ROTATION

North Atlantic Ocean. It carries warm water from the Gulf of Mexico to the Atlantic coasts of Europe. The Gulf Stream brings milder temperatures to Florida and to states along the East Coast. It also brings heat to northern Europe. Without the Gulf Stream, northern Europe would have colder temperatures.

density: a measure of how closely packed items are.

global conveyor belt: a system that moves deep ocean currents around the globe.

WORDS TO KNOW

Sailors first observed the Gulf Stream in the 1500s. Much later, Benjamin Franklin (1706–1790) took an interest in the current. Franklin was a writer and a scientist. On separate sea voyages, Franklin took notes on the air and water temperatures of the current. In 1786, Franklin used his data to make the first map of the Gulf Stream.

DEEP OCEAN CURRENTS

Deep ocean currents are created by density and temperature. Think about making a glass of chocolate milk. After you squirt the syrup in the milk, the syrup sinks. This is because the chocolate syrup is denser than milk. Ocean water is a lot like this glass of chocolate milk. Cold ocean water is denser than warm ocean water. Since it is denser, cold water sinks to the bottom of the sea. Warm water rises to the top because it is less dense.

As water rises or sinks, deep ocean currents are put into motion—part of the global conveyor belt. Unlike a conveyor belt in a factory that moves goods, this conveyor belt helps maintain the earth's climate. It gets the job done by mixing warm and cold ocean currents, spreading heat around the globe.

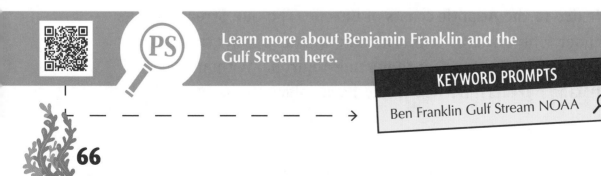

(PS) Learn more about Benjamin Franklin and the Gulf Stream here.

KEYWORD PROMPTS

Ben Franklin Gulf Stream NOAA

THEN & NOW

THEN: In 1998, rising sea temperatures caused 50 percent of the Great Barrier Reef in Australia to be bleached.

NOW: Some scientists think that coral bleaching caused by global warming will eventually destroy most coral reefs.

coral bleaching: coral that turns white, indicating it is ill and dying.

global warming: an increase in the average temperature of the earth's atmosphere, enough to cause climate change.

WORDS TO KNOW

The global conveyor belt begins near the North Pole. Water near the North Pole is colder and saltier than water near the equator. When the cold water sinks, the warm water from the equator takes its place. The cold water then moves toward the equator. Eventually, the cold water will warm up and return to the surface. How long does one trip around the earth take? Scientists do not know for sure. Some scientists believe that it could take up to 500 years or longer.

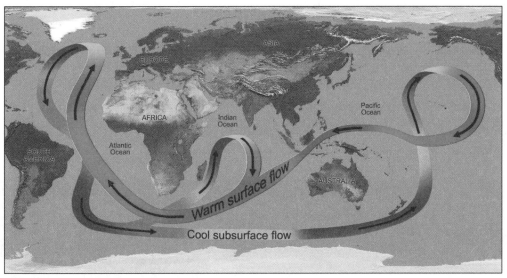

THE GLOBAL CONVEYOR BELT
CREDIT: NASA/JPL

Some scientists are worried about the global conveyor belt because the earth is getting hotter. The ocean soaks up most of this extra heat. Rising ocean temperatures could slow down the global conveyor belt. How? At the poles, sea ice is melting. Ice is not as salty as the ocean, so the melting ice makes the ocean less salty. This could slow down deep ocean currents.

Changes in deep ocean currents would affect the world's climate and produce more extreme weather. North America could have more floods and wildfires. Scientists are continuing to study the impact of melting sea ice and climate change. In the future, they hope to better understand how this system works.

What can you do to help the oceans stay in balance? Find out in the next chapter!

? CONSIDER AND DISCUSS

It's time to consider and discuss: Why is the ocean an important part of the earth's weather and climate?

RARE!

Off the coastline of Bermuda is a new ocean zone with a unique ecosystem. In 2018, scientists named this region the rariphotic zone, or the rare light zone. It extends from 400 to 1,000 feet below the ocean surface. Using submersibles and remote-control vehicles, scientists have already discovered 100 new species of marine life there!

Do you want to explore the deep reef? You can go on a dive with scientists to the deep reef here.

KEYWORD PROMPTS

Smithsonian ocean portal 🔍

PROJECT!

TEST A HYDROMETER

Differences in water density and temperature affect ocean currents. Scientists use a tool called a hydrometer **to measure the density of liquids. Make a simple hydrometer to learn how this works.**

SUPPLIES

* ✳ science journal and pencil
* ✳ nondrying modeling clay
* ✳ 2 straws
* ✳ 2 clear glasses
* ✳ water
* ✳ 2 rubber bands
* ✳ table salt

1 Start a scientific method worksheet in your science journal to record your data. Which straw will sink deeper?

2 Take a marble size-piece of clay, roll it into a ball, and press it to the end of a straw. Repeat this step for the second straw. These are your hydrometers, tools that can measure the density of liquid.

WHAT KIND OF HAIR DO OCEANS HAVE?

Wavy.

3 Fill both water glasses three-quarters full of water. Place one straw in each glass. Put a rubber band around each glass to mark the waterline.

4 Use a spoon to add salt to one glass. Keep adding salt until you notice a change in the hydrometer. What happens? Write down your observations and compare them to your prediction. Which is denser, salt water or tap water?

TRY THIS! Use the hydrometer to test the density of other liquids in your home, such as juice or dish soap.

WORDS TO KNOW

hydrometer: a tool for measuring the density of liquids.

SUPPLIES

* * science journal and pencil
* * 2 clear glasses
* * water
* * red and blue food coloring (do not use candy food coloring)

PROJECT!

WATER HOLDS HEAT

Does water really hold heat? Do a water experiment to study if this is true!

1 Create a scientific method worksheet in your science journal and write down a prediction. What do you think will happen when you add food coloring to the glass of hot water?

2 Fill a glass with cold tap water and place it in the refrigerator for about 10 minutes. Then, place this glass on a counter. Fill the second glass with hot tap water.

3 Add a few drops of blue food coloring to the glass with cold water and a few drops of red food coloring to the glass with hot water. Do not stir either glass.

4 Write down your observations and compare your results with your prediction. What happens to the food coloring as the water sits for 10 minutes? An hour?

WHAT IS HAPPENING? Everything, including you, is made up of tiny particles called **molecules**. The food coloring moves faster in warmer water than cold water because the molecules spread out more quickly in warm water.

70

WORDS TO KNOW

molecule: a group of atoms, which are the smallest particles of matter.

PROJECT!

CONVECTION CURRENT EXPERIMENT

Try this experiment to see how heat moves between warm and cold currents.

1 Create a scientific method worksheet in your science journal and write down a prediction. What do you think will happen when you turn the glass of cold water upside down over the glass of hot water?

2 Mark one glass "hot" and one glass "cold" with the masking tape and marker.

3 Fill one glass with hot water, add a drop of red food coloring, and stir. Fill the second glass with cold water, add a drop of blue food coloring, and stir. Place the glass with hot water on the baking sheet.

4 Place the piece of plastic over the glass of cold water to create a seal. Press firmly. Turn the glass upside down and slide it over the glass of hot water. Slowly remove the plastic. This step is tricky. It might take you a few tries to get it right. Just mop up the mess and try again!

5 What happens? Record your results. Compare them with your prediction. Was your hypothesis correct?

SUPPLIES
* science journal and pencil
* masking tape
* marker
* 2 empty spice containers
* water
* red and blue food coloring
* baking sheet (to catch drips)
* heavy piece of plastic
* dish towel

TRY THIS! Repeat the experiment above, but this time place the glass of hot water over the glass of cold water. Do you think your results will be different? What did you learn about the density of warm water compared to the density of cold water?

HURRICANE IN A JAR

Hurricanes are powerful ocean storms with a rapidly whirling spiral of air or water in the center called a vortex. Storms are fueled by warm ocean water—they suck up heat and moisture from the ocean. You can create a powerful storm right in your kitchen.

SUPPLIES

* ✳ science journal and pencil
* ✳ clear water bottle
* ✳ water
* ✳ dish soap
* ✳ vinegar

1 Create a scientific method worksheet in your science journal and write down a prediction. What do you think will happen when you swirl the water in the bottle?

2 Fill the bottle three-quarters full of tap water. Add a squirt of dish soap to the jar and a drop or two of vinegar. Screw the lid on tightly.

3 Swirl the bottle quickly. Then, stop suddenly and put the bottle down.

4 Write your observations in your science journal and compare your results with your prediction. Were you able to create a vortex?

TRY THIS! Repeat this experiment using **opaque** soap. Add the soap first and then the water. Let the water run out of the jar until the bubbles disappear. Add a drop of food coloring. Shake and spin. What happens?

WORDS TO KNOW

vortex: a rotating column of water or air.

opaque: not clear, so you can't see through it.

CHAPTER 6

CONSERVATION CHALLENGE

Although we do not know everything about the ocean yet, we do know that it's in trouble. If you walk along a beach almost anywhere on Earth, you'll see trash. Plastic bottles, fishing lines, toothbrushes, and fast-food containers do not belong in the ocean. And some pollution we can't see—it comes from sources such as homes and cars.

All of this pollution hurts the plants and animals that depend on the ocean for survival. And since the health of the ocean is connected to the health of the entire planet, it's important to try to keep the ocean as healthy as possible. Let's find out more about these threats and how we can help.

 INVESTIGATE!

How do you think people can better protect the oceans?

WORDS TO KNOW

microplastic: a tiny piece of plastic less than a quarter of an inch big.

PROBLEM: GARBAGE

In 1997, oceanographer Charles Moore discovered a swirling mass of trash that came to be known as the Great Pacific Garbage Patch. This is located in the Pacific Ocean in a current known as the North Pacific Gyre. The current flows between North America and Japan.

DID YOU KNOW?

More than 80 percent of the pollution in the ocean comes from the land.

There are four more garbage patches in the ocean. All this plastic is making the ocean sick. As decades pass, the wind, waves, and sun break down the plastic into tinier and tinier pieces called microplastic.

TRASH ON A SINGAPORE BEACH
CREDIT: VAIDEHI SHAH (CC BY 2.0)

Imagine what life is like for marine life. Some fish, sea mammals, and birds mistake the pieces of trash for food. When animals eat the plastic, they can become ill and even die. People who eat a lot of seafood can ingest this microplastic, too.

SOLUTION: REDUCE, REUSE, RECYCLE

You can help reduce ocean pollution. Work with a group in your area to reduce trash. Organize a cleanup in your local park or neighborhood! Every piece of trash that you pick up makes a difference. It's one less piece of trash that makes its way to the ocean.

You also can participate in a beach cleanup. Did you know that the state of California allows groups to adopt beaches? The group must pick up trash from the beach at least three times a year. Look for a program like this near you.

How about cutting back on the amount of trash that you create? Think carefully before you buy things. Instead of buying bottled water, use a refillable bottle or a water fountain. Try repairing an item before you buy a new one. Give a used toy or game to a friend instead of throwing it away.

WHY DID THE CAT GO SWIMMING IN THE OCEAN?

It wanted to be an octo-pus.

PROBLEM: GLOBAL WARMING

Have you ever been in a greenhouse? The glass windows trap the sun's heat so the air inside is much warmer than outside. The atmosphere around the earth works the same way.

OCEANS AND SEAS!

A group of gases in the atmosphere trap heat from the sun. They are called greenhouse gases. During the last few centuries, the level of greenhouse gases in the atmosphere has risen because people are burning more and more fossil fuels to power machines and other technologies. The extra gas causes the earth to heat up, which is global warming. The extra heat in the earth's atmosphere is then soaked up by the ocean.

Warmer ocean temperatures affect ocean life and cause acid levels to rise. This is called ocean acidification. When acid levels are high, marine life such as shellfish become stressed. Their skeletons and shells become thin and weak.

DID YOU KNOW?

If Arctic ice continues to melt at current rates, it may be possible to sail over the North Pole by 2030.

Warmer ocean temperatures are also a problem for coral reefs. Corals depend on algae living in their tissues to make food. When the ocean is too warm, the algae cannot make food. Corals then starve and lose their bright colors until only their white skeletons are left. This is called coral bleaching.

(PS) Calculate your impact on the environment with this online calculator.

KEYWORD PROMPTS

EPA kids calculator 🔍

Coral bleaching is a huge threat to biodiversity, because reefs support a quarter of all marine life. More than 70 percent of the coral reefs in the world have been affected by warming ocean temperatures, including the Great Barrier Reef in Australia. At 1,400 miles, it's the largest coral reef in the world. More than 1,500 species of fish and 400 species of coral live here. But this reef has been damaged by coral bleaching. Today, more than 90 percent of the reef is damaged.

EXAMPLE OF HEALTHY CORALS (LEFT) AND BLEACHED CORALS (RIGHT)

SOLUTION: CUT BACK

You can reduce carbon dioxide in the environment in many ways. Ride your bike, walk, or take the bus whenever possible. When you do need to take the car, make a list of errands that you can complete in one trip. This will cut down on gas.

THEN & NOW

THEN: The Ocean Conservancy is an international group that works to protect oceans. It has collected more than 228 million pounds of trash since 1985.

NOW: In 2018, inventor Boyan Slat (1994–) will launch machines that trap ocean plastic. He hopes to clean up 50 percent of the Great Pacific Garbage Patch in five years.

You can reduce energy use in your home. Remember to turn off lights when you leave a room. Did you know your home has electrical vampires? Hair dryers, phone chargers, toaster ovens, and other gadgets suck energy out of outlets even if they are turned off. Unplug them when you're not using them.

Much work still needs to be done to keep our oceans clean and healthy. You can help! By working with friends and your local community, you can make a difference in the lives of the plants, animals, and humans that rely on the oceans for survival.

CONSIDER AND DISCUSS

It's time to consider and discuss: How do you think people can better protect the oceans?

PS

Learn more about how you can help the environment at this NASA website.

KEYWORD PROMPTS

climate kids help NASA

ACIDIC OCEANS

With a few materials, you can learn what happens to shells in acidic water.

SUPPLIES

* science journal and pencil
* 4 to 6 clam or mussel shells
* colander
* kitchen towel
* 2 mixing bowls
* water
* measuring cups
* white vinegar
* masking tape
* pen

1 Start a scientific method worksheet and write a prediction in your science journal. What will happen to shells in acidic water?

2 Pour the shells into the colander. Rinse, scrub, and dry the shells thoroughly. Set to one side.

3 Fill one bowl with 1 cup of water. Fill the second bowl with half a cup of vinegar and half a cup of water. Use the masking tape and pen to label the bowl with vinegar.

4 Place the same type of shells in both bowls. What happens? Write down your observations in your science journal

WHAT IS HAPPENING? Shells are made of calcium carbonate. Vinegar is an acid. The vinegar removes the carbon from the shells. The carbon combines with oxygen to make carbon dioxide. The bubbles that you see are carbon dioxide. When no carbon is left in the shell, the bubbles disappear.

TRY THIS! Do this experiment with different acids in your fridge such as cola or pickle juice. Try using an antacid such as Tums instead of shells. What happens?

CLEANING UP AN OIL SPILL

Can you clean up an oil spill? Try this activity to find out.

1 Start a scientific method worksheet in your science journal. What do you think will happen to the feather when it is dipped in oil?

2 Fill the container halfway with tap water. Add a few drops of food coloring and mix with the spoon.

3 Add 2 tablespoons of vegetable oil to the middle of the container. Shake the bowl slightly to create a wave. Write down your observations. Does the oil sink, float, or mix in?

4 Dip the feather into the bowl. Set the feather on the plate. What happens to the feather when it gets oil on it? What does it feel like? Use the magnifying glass to look at the feather more closely. Write down your observations. Based on your observations, how would oil affect a bird?

SUPPLIES

* ✳ science journal and pencil
* ✳ plastic container
* ✳ water
* ✳ blue food coloring
* ✳ spoon
* ✳ vegetable oil
* ✳ craft feather
* ✳ plate
* ✳ magnifying glass
* ✳ dish soap
* ✳ salt

DID YOU KNOW?

Sea cucumbers help to keep the ocean clean. They eat sand to find food and poop out clean sand!

ANIMALS AND PLANTS UNDER THREAT

Many ocean plants and animals are at risk of disappearing forever. Habitat loss is one reason. A natural event such as a landslide or earthquake can change or even destroy habitats. People are also responsible for habitat loss. One way people hurt habitats is through a type of fishing called trawling. Trawling uses heavy rollers to drag huge metal nets along the bottom of the ocean. This can damage the seabed if the nets tear up plant roots and destroy animal homes, corals, and sponges. Trawling can also stirs up the sand, gravel, and mud on the sea floor. This sediment blocks the sunlight that plants need for photosynthesis, which then affects the entire marine food chain. In 2006, the United States banned trawling off its Pacific Coast. Many other countries have banned trawling, but habitat loss due to trawling is still an ongoing challenge.

5 Try to clean the feather with different substances. Use cold water, hot water, and water with dish soap. Before you begin, write another prediction. Which method will work best?

TRY THIS! Add a teaspoon of salt to the bowl of tap water. Repeat the experiment. How do your results compare?

WORDS TO KNOW

trawling: a type of fishing that involves dragging equipment along the bottom of the ocean.

81

PROJECT!

AN OCEAN ADVENTURE

Write your own ocean adventure. Fill in the blanks to create a story.

- **Nouns:** fish, octopus, shark, kelp, coral, ecosystem, ice, continents, volcano, wave, lava, tide

- **Verbs:** climb, swim, dive, ate, lift, crawl, smell, hear, explore, wonder, study, change

- **Adjectives:** small, tiny, shimmer, beautiful, dark, blue, red, hard, hot, scary, salty, huge

- **Adverbs:** bravely, quietly, quickly, silently, carefully, slowly, happily, easily, nicely, loudly, happily, sadly

_____ lived at the bottom of the ocean with a _____ and
   NAME   NOUN

two _____. _____ was in charge of _____ the underwater volcanoes
     NOUNS   NAME   VERB

and feeding the _____ _____.
                   ADJECTIVE   NOUN

One _____ morning, a huge _____ _____ _____ floated by his/
    ADJECTIVE   NOUN   ADVERB   VERB

her house.

_____ decided to say hello and together they _____ _____ the seabed.
 NAME   ADVERB   VERB

They saw _____ _____. They _____ gathered _____ and
        ADJECTIVE NOUN   ADVERB   NOUN

ate _____ _____. The two new friends were having such a terrific time
   ADJECTIVE NOUN

that they did not notice the ocean was getting hotter.

Suddenly, _____ heard a terrific sound. It was the _____. It _____
      NAME   NOUN   ADVERB

sent _____ _____ into the water. The friends decided to _____. When
    ADJECTIVE NOUN   VERB

they were far away from the _____, they rested under a _____ _____.
                      NOUN   ADJECTIVE NOUN

What an exciting day! They wondered what they would _____ tomorrow.
                                           VERB

A

absorb: to soak up.

adapt: to make changes to better survive in an environment.

algae: a simple organism found in water that is like a plant but without roots, stems, or leaves.

alginate: a seaweed extract that makes foods thicker.

atmosphere: a layer of gas surrounding the earth.

B

bacteria: tiny organisms found in animals, plants, soil, and water.

ballast: something used to make a ship more stable, such as water or sand.

bay: a body of water that is surrounded by land on three sides.

BCE: put after a date, BCE stands for Before Common Era and counts down to zero. CE stands for Common Era and counts up from zero. These non-religious terms correspond to BC and AD. This book was printed in 2018 CE.

biodiversity: the range of living things in an area.

bioluminescent: describes an organism that produces its own light.

C

camouflage: colors or patterns that animals use to blend in with their environment.

carbon dioxide: a gas formed by the burning of fossil fuels, the rotting of plants and animals, and the breathing out of animals or humans.

cargo ship: a ship used to carry goods and materials from one port to another.

cephalopod: a class of mollusks, including the squid and octopus, characterized by their ability to fill their bodies with water and quickly let it out in order to move.

Challenger Deep: the deepest known point in the earth's seabed at the bottom of the Mariana Trench in the Pacific Ocean.

circumference: the distance around the edge of a circle.

civilization: a community of people that is advanced in art, science, and government.

classification system: a way of organizing things in groups.

climate: weather patterns over a long period of time.

climate change: a change in long-term weather patterns, which can happen through natural or man-made processes.

clockwise: the direction that follows the hands of a clock.

compass: a device that uses a magnet to show which direction is north.

condensation: the process of a gas cooling down and changing into a liquid.

constellation: a group of stars that form a pattern.

continent: one of the earth's largest land areas, including Africa, Antarctica, Asia, Australia, Europe, North America, and South America.

coral bleaching: coral that turns white, indicating it is ill and dying.

coral reef: an underwater ecosystem that grows in warm ocean waters and is home to millions of creatures. Corals are tiny animals that build shells around themselves.

counterclockwise: the direction that goes opposite to the hands of a clock.

crustacean: a type of animal, such as a crab or lobster, that lives mainly in water. It has several pairs of legs and its body is made up of sections covered in a hard outer shell.

culture: a group of people who share beliefs and a way of life.

current: the steady flow of water or air in one direction.

D

dead reckoning: a method of determining a ship's position by using a previously determined position and the distance traveled.

dense: when something is tightly packed in its space.

density: a measure of how closely packed items are.

dike: a long earthen wall built to prevent flooding.

dissolve: to mix with a liquid and become part of the liquid.

E

ecosystem: a community of living and nonliving things and their environment. Living things are plants, animals, and insects. Nonliving things are soil, rocks, and water.

equator: an invisible line around the earth that is an equal distance from the North and South Poles.

evaporation: the process where a liquid heats up and changes into a gas.

F

fathom: a measurement of about 6 feet.

float: the little bubble on kelp filled with gas that helps keep the kelp afloat.

food chain: a community of animals and plants where each is eaten by another higher up in the chain.

fossil fuel: a source of energy that comes from plants and animals that lived millions of years ago.

G

geography: the features of a place, such as mountains and rivers.

global conveyor belt: a system that moves deep ocean currents around the globe.

global warming: an increase in the average temperature of the earth's atmosphere, enough to cause climate change.

goods: things to use or sell.

GPS: stands for Global Positioning System, a network of satellites that can be used to find your location on Earth.

greenhouse gas: a gas such as carbon dioxide that traps the sun's energy.

H

habitat: an area where certain plants and animals live together.

holdfast: a structure that anchors kelp to the seafloor.

horizontal: straight across from side to side.

hydrometer: a tool for measuring the density of liquids.

hydrothermal vent: a crack on the seafloor where water heated by volcanic activity gushes out.

I

invertebrate: an animal without a backbone.

K

krill: small crustaceans found in all the world's oceans.

L

lagoon: salt water that is separated from the ocean by a barrier such as a reef.

latitude: imaginary lines around the earth that measure a position north or south of the equator.

longitude: imaginary lines running through the North and South Poles that indicate where you are on the globe.

M

magma: hot, flowing rock below the surface of the earth.

mammal: an animal such as a human, dog, or cat. Mammals are born live, feed milk to their young, and usually have hair or fur.

marine: having to do with the ocean.

marine snow: what falls to the ocean floor when marine animals die or excrete waste.

microplastic: a tiny piece of plastic less than a quarter of an inch big.

midnight zone: an area of the ocean between 3,000 feet below the surface and the seafloor.

mine: to dig something out of the ground.

mineral: a solid, nonliving substance found in nature, such as gold, salt, or copper.

molecule: a group of atoms, which are the smallest particles of matter.

monsoon: a wind system in Asia that brings heavy rains for one part of the year and almost no rain the rest of the year.

Morse code: a code in which letters are represented by combinations of dots and dashes, or long and short signals of light or sound.

mythology: a collection of traditional stories, either truthful or exaggerated, that are often focused on historical events.

N

naturalist: a person who studies nature.

natural disaster: a natural event, such as a fire or flood, that causes great damage.

natural resource: something found in nature that is useful to humans, such as water to drink, trees to burn and build with, and fish to eat.

navigate: to find your way from one place to another.

nonrenewable: a resource such as coal that, once used, is gone forever.

nori: dried seaweed often used to wrap sushi.

Norse: people from Denmark, Norway, and Sweden.

Northern Hemisphere: the half of the earth north of the equator.

nutrients: substances in food, water, and soil that living things need to live and grow.

O

ocean acidification: the absorption of too much carbon dioxide by oceans, causing acid levels to rise.

ocean: a large body of salt water that surrounds the earth's continents.

oceanographer: a scientist who studies the ocean.

oil rig: a platform with drilling equipment used to extract oil from the ocean floor.

opaque: not clear, so you can't see through it.

organism: a living thing, such as an animal or a plant.

oxygen: a gas in the air that animals and humans need to breathe to stay alive.

P

periscope: a long tube with two mirrors used in submarines to see above the surface of the ocean.

photosynthesis: the process plants use to turn sunlight, carbon dioxide, and water into food.

phytoplankton: tiny organisms that are at the base of ocean food chains.

port: a place where ships can load and unload.

predator: an animal that hunts other animals for food.

prey: an animal that is killed by another for food.

pulley: a simple machine consisting of a wheel with a grooved rim that a rope or chain is pulled through to help lift up a load.

R

reef: an underwater structure made of corals, sand, and rock.

renewable: a resource such as wind that people can never run out of.

rotation: a turn all the way around.

S

salt water: water with a large amount of salt in it.

sea: a large body of salt water that is mostly surrounded by land.

seaweed: a type of plant that grows in the ocean.

sediment: bits of rock, sand, or dirt.

simple machine: a tool, such as a lever, wedge, wheel and axle, pulley, screw, or inclined plane, that uses one movement to complete work.

species: a group of living things that are closely related and can produce young.

stipe: a long, flexible stalk.

submersible: a boat that can go below the surface of the water.

sunlight zone: an area of the ocean from the surface to where light doesn't reach, usually about 600 feet below.

T

technology: the tools, methods, and systems used to solve a problem or do work.

tidal: having to do with the daily rise and fall of ocean water.

tidepool: a pool of ocean water that remains after the tide goes out.

trade: the buying, selling, or exchange of goods and services between countries.

trawling: a type of fishing that involves dragging equipment along the bottom of the ocean.

turbine: a machine that produces energy from moving liquid or air.

twilight zone: a dim area of the ocean that begins at about 600 feet below the surface.

V

vortex: a rotating column of water or air.

W

water cycle: the continuous movement of water from the earth to the clouds and back again.

water vapor: the gas form of water.

weather: the temperature, rain, and wind conditions of an area, which change daily.

Z

zone: an area of the ocean based on depth.

METRIC CONVERSIONS

Use this chart to find the metric equivalents to the English measurements in this book. If you need to know a half measurement, divide by two. If you need to know twice the measurement, multiply by two. How do you find a quarter measurement? How do you find three times the measurement?

English	Metric
1 inch	2.5 centimeters
1 foot	30.5 centimeters
1 yard	0.9 meter
1 mile	1.6 kilometers
1 pound	0.5 kilogram
1 teaspoon	5 milliliters
1 tablespoon	15 milliliters
1 cup	237 milliliters

BOOKS

Berkenkamp, Lauri. *Discover the Oceans: The World's Largest Ecosystem.* Nomad Press, 2009.

Fleming, Candace. *Giant Squid.* Roaring Brook Press, 2016.

Gibson, Karen Bush. *Marine Biology: Cool Women Who Dive.* Nomad Press, 2016.

Hestermann, Bethanie, and Josh Hestermann. *Marine Science for Kids: Exploring and Protecting Our Watery World, Includes Cool Careers and 21 Activities.* Chicago Review Press, 2017.

Mooney, Carla. *Explore Rivers and Ponds! With 25 Great Projects.* Nomad Press, 2012.

Yasuda, Anita. *Explore Water! 25 Great Projects, Activities, Experiments.* Nomad Press, 2011.

WEBSITES

Discovery Kids: discoverykids.com

Ducksters—Oceans for Kids: ducksters.com/geography/oceans.php

EPA—Oceans and Coasts: epa.gov/oceans-and-coasts

Kids Do Ecology—Marine: kids.nceas.ucsb.edu/biomes/marine.html

National Geographic Kids—Ocean Facts!
natgeokids.com/uk/discover/geography/general-geography/ocean-facts

NOAA—National Ocean Service: oceanservice.noaa.gov

NOAA—Coral Reef Conservation Program: coralreef.noaa.gov

NOAA—National Marine Sanctuaries: sanctuaries.noaa.gov/education/fun/welcome.html

Ocean Portal—Find Your Blue: ocean.si.edu

Science Kids—Fun Ocean Facts: sciencekids.co.nz/sciencefacts/earth/oceans.html

Secrets at Sea: secretsatsea.org/main.html

USGS—The Water Cycle-Oceans: water.usgs.gov/edu/watercycleoceans.html

SCIENCE MUSEUMS AND AQUARIUMS

American Museum of Natural History:
New York, New York
amnh.org/exhibitions/water-h2o-life

Aquarium of the Bay:
San Francisco, California
aquariumofthebay.org/teachers/teacher-resources/teacher-resource-guides

Aquarium of the Pacific:
Long Beach, California
aquariumofpacific.org

Georgia Aquarium:
Atlanta, Georgia
georgiaaquarium.org

Marine Science Center:
Ponce Inlet, Florida
marinesciencecenter.com

Monterey Bay Aquarium:
Monterey, California
montereybayaquarium.org/education/classroom-resources/ocean-explorer-guides

The Maritime Aquarium:
Norwalk, Connecticut
maritimeaquarium.org

Woods Hole Oceanographic Institution:
Woods Hole, Massachusetts
whoi.edu

QR CODE GLOSSARY

ESSENTIAL QUESTIONS

Introduction: Why do you think Earth is nicknamed the Blue Planet?

Chapter 1: What three objects in your home came from an ocean resource?

Chapter 2: What methods did sailors use in the past
to find their way on the open ocean?

Chapter 3: How do scientists determine ocean zones?

Chapter 4: Which ocean zone do most plants live in and why?

Chapter 5: Why is the ocean an important part of the earth's weather and climate?

Chapter 6: How do you think people can better protect the oceans?

INDEX

I
Indian Ocean, 2–3, 4, 29, 39
invasive species, 23

K
kelp, iv, 51, 52–53, 55–57

M
maps, 4, 8, 27–28, 29, 33, 35, 67
Mariana Trench, 32, 42, 45
marine snow, 42–43
medicines, 19, 20, 21
Mediterranean Sea, 7–8
midnight zone, 39, 42–43
minerals, 18–19, 24–25
Moore, Charles, 74

N
navigation, 26–28, 31, 33, 36–37
Northwest Passage, 35

O
Ocean Conservancy, 78
oceans and seas
  animals in. *See* animals
  conservation and
    protection of, 73–81
  definitions and
    descriptions of, 2–4, 7–9
  humans and. *See* humans
  plants in. *See* plants
  pollution in, 16, 54, 73–78, 80–81
  resources from, 14–25. *See also* animals; plants
  role and importance of
    study of, 6–7. *See also* exploration
  weather, climate and, 3, 54, 62–72, 75–78
  zones of, 39–45, 51, 68

octopuses, 29, 39, 41
oil and gas, 16–17, 76, 77, 80–81
oxygen, 50, 51–52, 58–59

P
Pacific Ocean, 2–3, 4, 32, 35, 39, 53, 74
photosynthesis, 51–52, 81
phytoplankton, v, 51–52, 59
plants. *See also specific plants*
  common or typical, iv–v, 50–61
  exploration of, 1, 13, 28, 32
  food for/from, 19–20, 23, 50, 51–52, 54, 60–61, 76, 81
  habitats or zones for, 41, 51, 81
  invasive, 23
  oxygen from, 50, 51–52, 58–59
  pollution affecting, 73
  resources from, 19–20, 21, 50, 51–52, 58–61
pollution, 16, 54, 73–78, 80–81
Pomponi, Shirley, 20

Q
questions to investigate, 10, 20, 32, 43, 54, 68, 78

R
rare light/rariphotic zone, 68
resources, ocean, 14–25. *See also* animals; plants

S
salt, 18, 24–25
Sargasso Sea, 9
scientific method/journal, 10, 12–13
seagrasses, v, 51, 53–54, 61
sea lions, 39
seaweed, 9, 19–20, 21, 51, 60–61
sharks, 3, 7, 39–40, 46
ships/shipping, 18, 22–23, 26–29, 31, 63
Slat, Boyan, 78
Southern Ocean, 2, 4
sponges, 1, 20
squids, 30, 42–43, 47
stick charts, 28, 33
storms, 3, 63, 72
submarines/submersibles, 30–32, 45, 68
sunlight zone, 39–40, 51

T
temperature, 4, 29, 32, 49, 63–72, 75–78
Thunder Horse oil rig, 17
tides/tidal energy, 15
trawling, 81
tube worms, 31, 42
twilight zone, 39, 41

V
vampire squids, 42–43
volcanoes, 3, 8, 32, 48–49

W
water cycle, 62, 63–64
weather and climate, 3, 54, 62–72, 75–78
whales, v, 40
whale shark, 3

Z
zones, 39–45, 51, 68

90